Tell My Son, Thank You

By Tiara Nicole

PenFire Publishing

Penfire Publishing
Kansas City, MO
www.spokenpurpose.com/PenFirePublishing

Copyright © 2021
All rights reserved. No part of this book may be reproduced, scanned, or distributed in any printed or electronic form, including information storage and retrieval systems, without permission. Please do not participate in or encourage piracy of copyrighted materials in violation of the author's rights.

Please purchase only authorized editions.

First Edition: January 2022
ISBN: 978-1-952838-09-5

This book is a work of fiction. Names, characters, places, dates, and incidents are products of the author's imagination, or are used fictitiously, satirically, or as parody. Any resemblance to actual persons, living or dead, business establishments, events, or locales is entirely coincidental.

10 9 8 7 6 5 4 3 2 1

Design, Layout, Edits: Sheri Purpose Hall
Cover Art: Tiara Patterson

Terry and Lisa's daughter
Geneva and Michael's bonus child
Candice and Quinten's sister
Florene and Maurice's favorite
Gracie's Baby
Tristian's Mama

Tiara Nicole
Poet

Table of Contents

Some of these poems are not suitable for children. Profanity and Explicit Content Parental discretion is advised.

Urban Tales 8
   In My Hood 10
   Sunshine 11
   The Ho That Never Made It To Housewife 12
   Automated System #1 14
LOVE 15
   Type Of Love 17
   Pep Talk (Good Girl) 19
   Sounds Like Shit 21
   Automated System #5 23
Dedications 25
   To Infinity 26
   Automated System 3 29
   Especially Different 32

Urban Tales
Based on a true story somewhere

In My Hood

There's a billboard that reads
AMERICA'S MOST WANTED
Blocking the sunshine
Making it hard to see where
She's walking.
But, before you start talking,
This is *her* neighborhood.

There's no such thing as
Pixie and dust and fairies.
The closest she gets to
Flowers in the yard is dandelions.
And those ain't nothing but weeds
The closest she gets to a role model
Is the old man on the radio asking

                         "Have you seen her?"

Oh well, she lives this.
And since nobody gon pack up
Her rags and move her to Beverly
She has to endure:
>   *Potholes / Gunshot holes in classroom windows /*
>   *Knockoff shoes and clothes sold on every other corner*
>   *for the low / And don't forget the crackhead ho's.*

She lives this.
She don't watch much tv.
She just goes outside
And while stepping on
Cigarette butts
Just for fun,
She watches the stories.

Sunshine

"Ain't no sunshine when she's gone, only darkness every day, ain't no sunshine when she's gone, and she's always gone too long any time she goes away."

"I wonder this time where she's gone, tell me if she's gone to stay, ain't no sunshine when she's gone, and she's always gone too long any time she goes away."

–Bill Withers

This girl, I call her Sunshine because I don't know her name. Her claim to fame isn't a college degree. In her mind, her family has to eat but should that really be her job? She is only a teen, more like a preteen, the oldest of three.

She chose this hustle because she watches too much damn T.V. She's got every hood novel in the library committed to memory. Her mind's warped into thinking things that she shouldn't be thinking at her age.

The Fairytale became a reality. The only actors in this little girl's life were her parents. Her mama was a junkie. Her daddy had three other families. The last time mama went out, she promised her it would be the last time, but baby girl refused to cry. She wiped her little brother's eyes and told them things would be fine in due time.

Things would be fine, and this fine led her to a life of crime. Sleeping in the beds of grown assed men because the beds they made had no consequence. She was headed to an early grave playing roles she became accustomed to. Everything from prostitute, to being her mama's pusher just to save her family.

If I could, I would rewrite her story; give her the childhood she's been missing because this little girl has been gone too long.

The Ho That Never Made It To Housewife

She was in love with a nigga that didn't want her heart. A lil bumping and grinding in the middle of the night while his wife was asleep was all that mattered.

Every time she closed her eyes, scattered traces of what it meant to be loved is what kept her going. A dream of a family; 2.5 kids and a husband that was hers from the beginning kept the noose from around her neck. But she was a wreck at times. Played connect the dots with the push-pin scars on her arms from shooting deadly venom. But that's not how the nightmare began; it started when she was young.

Her mama hid that she was selling her young daughter for cheap drugs from her fire baptized Grandma. The dope man taught her when she was nine how to keep the semen from getting in her eye. The pain every time a nigga twice her age thrust on top of her made her body numb.

Her tears became silent. And after the first time her mama slapped her for saying NO, it became a habit.
If you love me, you would…
is what she heard. But, not from some sixteen-year-old nigga trying to bust his first nut,
she heard it from her mother.

So, it was in the name of love that she did it. Even after her mama died, she kept doing it because, well, that was all she knew. But Grandmother wasn't dumb. She couldn't do anything about it but pray that her granddaughter would return home.

She was ready to bow out of the game gracefully. No longer

sharing her body with the man of another woman. But grandmother wasn't the only one that wasn't dumb. The woman of the man was well aware of what was going on. She didn't sleep as hard as he thought she did.

Police told grandmother that they found granddaughter killed by the woman she wanted to be; The wife. And while baby girl floated in blood, the husband's blood was scribed on the wall -

The Ho Never Made it To Housewife

Automated System #1

I wish Heaven had a phone or maybe even an automated system.
>Because every time I look in the sky,
>I'm not always talking to God.

For Granny press One:
    I miss the green beans and ham
    You would make on Sundays
    I miss the sweet potatoes
    Even though I never ate them
    I haven't found a bread pudding
    That comes close to yours
    I can sometimes smell
    The blueberry muffins
    You would bake
    After school for me
    I miss the times
    That you would sing off-key
>*You are my sunshine*
>*My only sunshine*
>*You make me happy*
>*When skies are grey*

    Your body was already
    Stiff and cold
    And I sang that song to you
    For the last time
    I wish I had said more
    I'd like to think you knew
    Even though it seemed
    Like your memory
    Failed you
    That I loved you beyond
    My own understanding
    You held me down
    Gave me love

              …I hope you're proud of me.

LOVE

While I was still trying to figure it out, I had moments when I wrote about it; the good, the bad, and everything in-between.

Type Of Love

I want that
Wake-up
In the middle of the night
With you on my mind -
                Type love
That
Baby was you busy?
If so, I can call you back
And you say
Naw, it's okay -
                Type love
That
You hang up
No, you hang up
Okay, on the count of three.
                Type love
That laugh together
Because neither one of us
Have any sense -
                Kind of love
I want that
Since
The first time I saw you
I knew it was
Something about you -
                Type love
That
Easy like Sunday morning
Gentle like a soft rain -
                Type love
I want that
                Safe love

That
                Refuge love

That
If I ain't got you
Is life really worth living?
    Type love

That
One day at a time
Only understood
Between us -
    Type love

That
As long as you are interested
I will be too –
    Type love

Pep Talk (Good Girl)

I'm a good girl with a lot to offer
I'm a good girl with a lot to offer
I can do just about anything
Above and under the sun
To make my man happy

It's what I tell myself when I wake up in the morning

I try to make myself believe it
When the fact is I don't
     I give
     I give
     I give
And get nothing in return

I'm smart with a good head on my shoulders. But it seems the only thing I'm good for is making the men in my life realize that the woman they should be with is the one
                                              before me.
When really, that chick did them scandalous, and that's how they found me.
                                      But now they're leaving.
And a new one comes along

I find myself relating their small mistakes to the big ones you made. I'm listening to slow songs trying to bounce back into the mood of love. I'm reading romance novels hoping that one of the men would fall out of the pages and into my lap so that I can breathe relationship again.

But you hurt me beyond measure, and now that I think on it, I should have never given you my treasure. You have invaded my thoughts with infatuation. You became the rhyme to my reason for insecurity.

I'm so used to the lie that I cant tell the truth. I want to believe that this one is real, but there I go again, relating small mistakes to the big ones you made.

But I am persuaded that before it's all said and done, my son will see me happy; will know what love is through the eyes of his mommy because…

I'm a good girl with a lot to offer
I'm a good girl with a lot to offer
I can do just about anything
Above and under the sun
To make my man happy

It's what I will keep telling myself In the morning
Until it comes true.

Sounds Like Shit

Listen,
I love you, really I do.
But I am a woman,
You have to let me be that.
You can't control my every move.

        Just because you
        See me talking
        To other dudes
        Don't mean I'm cheatin'.
        It's just conversation
        At the moment.

How his number
Got in my phone
I'm not sure.
He's not my type.
I mean, me fucking him
Would be like pigs flying.
I wouldn't fuck him
With another woman's pussy.
So what's that tell you?

        The only reason
        I didn't come home
        Is because I ran out of gas.
        You know how high that is!

I sent you straight to voicemail
Because my finger slipped.
And my battery was going dead.
That's the reason
I didn't call you back

        That dude you saw me
        In the car with
        Already has a girlfriend.
        Besides, what's that matter,

> You the one
> I'm coming home to

The only reason
I jumped in the shower
After coming from the club
With my girls
Is 'cause I smelled like smoke.
And besides that,
I had a long day at work.

> The only reason
> I go in the other room
> When I'm on the phone
> Is cause sometimes
> I have trouble hearing.

That text you read
Was from my cousin
And I promise
He was just playin'.

> Ron—
> I could have swore
> Yo middle name was Ronnie!
> I could have swore
> That it was you
> That bought this for me.

I don't think
Your mama would like me.
That's why
I'm not ready to meet her.

> Your birthday is today?
> I thought it
> Had already passed.

I ain't got to explain myself to you
Because you should trust me.

> *If this sounds like shit, I know.*
> *It's what I hear from you.*

Automated System #5

Because every time I look in the sky,
I'm not always talking to God.

For Sugabear Press Five:
        I know its past visiting hours
        But can I please bring you these flowers
        I said it for the first and last time
        At your funeral
        You're the main reason that I wish
        I had Magic's money
        I don't think it was done
        I think you was tired
        That beast of a cancer
        Brought you to your knees
        There was a lot I didn't tell you
        A lot that I kept to myself
        Because I've never really known
        How to express myself
        Without writing it down first
        You were the first one
        The only one I really
        Trusted to take care of her
        And you did what you could
        I try to imagine how
        Things would be now
        And I can't put it into words
                But she misses you
                I miss you
        As annoying as it was
        I miss the conversations that
        You would leave on my voicemail
        The random calls
        In the middle of the night
                Cause you dreamt
                With your eyes open

Tristian wouldn't be any good
I already know that
You were Mr Fix it
Even when I didn't
Want you to be
Sometimes I wish I still had
You going to bat for me
Got triggered the other day
Things left unsaid
Came back to the surface
Went to pick up the phone
And that's when it hit me

I wish heaven had a phone, or maybe even an automated system.
Because every time I look in the sky,
I'm not always talking to God.

Dedications

To Infinity

Did you ever know that you were my hero
You were everything I wish I could be
I can fly higher than an eagle
With you as the wind beneath my wings

I

Robert,
I love you and celebrate you for who you were.

Every time I close my eyes, I see you
Smiling
Cheesing
Calling me baby
Telling me when I get weak
You gon hold me down
Who's gon hold me now
Who's gon get mad
Right along with me
Who's gon help me
Raise my children
Who's gon be there
To tell that man
I'll cut you if you ever
Think about hurting her
You were my heart
The iron that sharpens
Kept me believing
Things wouldn't be
The way they are for long
I guess
I will never get my license
I'll never hear you say
The things that always made me smile

Though it's only been a short while
My life as I know it
Has been turned upside down

II

Robert,
I love you and celebrate you for who you are.

I told you the last time I talked to you that the next time I picked up my pen, I would really *put it down*. Stand proud in any place and say it's for the rest of my life that I'll love you. You were more than just my friend; you were my love. With all the things we went through, I would never have imagined that NOW I would look down on you and have to say goodbye. I'm trying not to cry, trying to be strong. But everything in me wishes that I could be where you are.

III

Robert,
I love you and celebrate your memory.

The life of any party
Could shake a tail feather
Better than any other
If I wanted to be mad at you
I couldn't
Can't forget who you were
What you are
A distant memory
You will never be
      -to infinity

IV

Robert,
I love you and celebrate you for who you made me.

You completed everything that was
  She | T | Tiara | The Future Mrs Bates III | Mrs Next

I'll miss you far more than any of these words can express. You always had a way of making me feel good about myself. And although a piece of me left with you on February 10th, you will always be my friend. I will keep the thoughts of yesteryear dear; hold you close and near. You made six of the 22 years I lived sweet.

I love you, RLB3. My best friend, you will always be; until the end of my time and beyond that. I call this relationship, Infinity.

Automated System 3

If heaven had a phone
> *Because every time I look in the sky,*
> *I'm not always talking to God.*

Press 3 for Uncle:
      I never called you by name
      You were just uncle
      My mamas only brother
      My favorite uncle
      No shade to my other uncles
      But the love I have for you
      Doesn't compare
      I love all of them in their own way
      But the way I loved you
> *You were my hero*
> *Larger than life*
> *Not just cause you stood*
> *At almost 7ft tall*

      You were a giant in my eyes

      You doubted a lot
      I heard it in your voice at times
      Spent the majority of your life
      On a cell block

      When they lost you
      In solitary confinement
      For what should have only been
      One week
      That turned into
      Six months
      I wish you could have seen the hell
      My mama and grandma raised
> *They didn't play 'bout you*
> *None of the women in*

        Our family did
You were
Still are
       Loved
       The favorite
Brings a slight tear
To my eye
Knowing you will never know
Never read in real time
Never see this
I didn't get a chance to say
       Goodbye
And it was never goodbye
It was always
       You know Uncle loves you
       Right
And I would just say
       Right
Missing you has new meaning now
The demons wouldn't leave you alone
You stayed running
Couldn't do the city
Small town worked
Better for you
More likely to stay out of trouble

I cherish the moments
I had you in close vicinity
The most
I never got to tell you that
       I get it
       I understand
       I can relate
I struggled with feeling like
I would never be enough
The only comfort
I have is saying
Rest in peace

And meaning it
You are finally free
From all the things
That had you bound
> You were alone
> Felt alone
> Died alone

It hurts
I loved you far more
Than you would ever know
The sun rose, set, and fell on you
I wish we could dance again
I wish I could hear you say
> Roll up niece

I wish heaven had a phone, or maybe even an automated system.
> *Because every time I look in the sky,*
> *I'm not always talking to God.*

Especially Different

He loves me
Especially different
He keeps me on my toes
Has brought me to my knees
And kept me there

It's been seven years
With a lifetime to go
We just getting started
I never knew love like this
Could exist

I tried just the other day
To remember what life was
Before I met him
Before I had any idea that
He would show up

                I drew a blank, couldn't remember

I know I had a life before
But those stories
Don't come close
To the memories
I'm creating with him now

It's the smile for me
It's telling me I'm the best
When what I did was simple
He loves me
Especially different

                The idea of affection made my skin crawl

But when he walks to me
With arms extended

My heart, it melts
He loves me,
Especially different

    He is the reflection of genuine affection

Asking me how I'm feeling
How my day was
If I'm happy
I remember the first time
I gave him a negative answer

    He just looked at me didn't say anything

Moments later, he returned
And with a glance
I acknowledge
And he says
I love you, mommy

    Smiling my from heart, I know he means it

He loves me
Especially different
He keeps me on my toes
Has brought me to my knees
And kept me there

I tried to think
Of what life was before
And I honestly can't remember
I can't see life
Without him in it

        Love you, Tristian

Tell My Son, Thank you is a collection of poetry I have written over the years. This is poetry that I thought I would never allow anyone to see. I hope that you enjoyed this collection. The next book, "Was It Something I Said?" will be released in 2022.

Tell him, thank you, the next time you see him because he is the reason!

                    Tiara Nicole